This Fishing Log Belongs To:

_____

LIFE IS ALWAYS

BETTER

WHEN I'M

FISHING

Fishing Log

Date: | **Time:**

Location/GPS:

Fishing Crew:

Weather

Conditions:

Air Temp:

Wind Speed:

Wind Direction:

Barometer:

Moon Phase:

Water

Temperature:

Depth:

Clarity:

Speed:

Direction:

Notes:

Tackle & Technique

Rod/Reel:

Bait:

Lures:

Fishing Method:

Notes:

Catch

Species	Length/Weight	Notes

Notes/Memories

_____

_____

_____

_____

_____

_____

Fishing Log

Date: | **Time:**

Location/GPS:

Fishing Crew:

Weather

Conditions:

Air Temp:

Wind Speed:

Wind Direction:

Barometer:

Moon Phase:

Water

Temperature:

Depth:

Clarity:

Speed:

Direction:

Notes:

Tackle & Technique

Rod/Reel:

Bait:

Lures:

Fishing Method:

Notes:

Catch

Species	Length/Weight	Notes

Notes/Memories

Fishing Log

Date: | **Time:**

Location/GPS:

Fishing Crew:

Weather

Conditions:

Air Temp:

Wind Speed:

Wind Direction:

Barometer:

Moon Phase:

Water

Temperature:

Depth:

Clarity:

Speed:

Direction:

Notes:

Tackle & Technique

Rod/Reel:

Bait:

Lures:

Fishing Method:

Notes:

Catch

Species	Length/Weight	Notes

Notes/Memories

Fishing Log

Date: | **Time:**

Location/GPS:

Fishing Crew:

Weather

Conditions:	
Air Temp:	
Wind Speed:	
Wind Direction:	
Barometer:	
Moon Phase:	

Water

Temperature:	
Depth:	
Clarity:	
Speed:	
Direction:	
Notes:	

Tackle & Technique

Rod/Reel:

Bait:

Lures:

Fishing Method:

Notes:

Catch

Species	Length/Weight	Notes

Notes/Memories

Fishing Log

Date: | **Time:**

Location/GPS:

Fishing Crew:

Weather

Conditions:

Air Temp:

Wind Speed:

Wind Direction:

Barometer:

Moon Phase:

Water

Temperature:

Depth:

Clarity:

Speed:

Direction:

Notes:

Tackle & Technique

Rod/Reel:

Bait:

Lures:

Fishing Method:

Notes:

Catch

Species	Length/Weight	Notes

Notes/Memories

Fishing Log

Date: | **Time:**

Location/GPS:

Fishing Crew:

Weather

Conditions:	
Air Temp:	
Wind Speed:	
Wind Direction:	
Barometer:	
Moon Phase:	

Water

Temperature:	
Depth:	
Clarity:	
Speed:	
Direction:	
Notes:	

Tackle & Technique

Rod/Reel:	
Bait:	
Lures:	
Fishing Method:	
Notes:	

Catch

Species	Length/Weight	Notes

Notes/Memories

Fishing Log

Date: | **Time:**

Location/GPS:

Fishing Crew:

Weather

Conditions:

Air Temp:

Wind Speed:

Wind Direction:

Barometer:

Moon Phase:

Water

Temperature:

Depth:

Clarity:

Speed:

Direction:

Notes:

Tackle & Technique

Rod/Reel:

Bait:

Lures:

Fishing Method:

Notes:

Catch

Species	Length/Weight	Notes

Notes/Memories

Fishing Log

Date: | **Time:**

Location/GPS:

Fishing Crew:

Weather

Conditions:

Air Temp:

Wind Speed:

Wind Direction:

Barometer:

Moon Phase:

Water

Temperature:

Depth:

Clarity:

Speed:

Direction:

Notes:

Tackle & Technique

Rod/Reel:

Bait:

Lures:

Fishing Method:

Notes:

Catch

Species	Length/Weight	Notes

Notes/Memories

Fishing Log

Date: **Time:**

Location/GPS:

Fishing Crew:

Weather

Conditions:	
Air Temp:	
Wind Speed:	
Wind Direction:	
Barometer:	
Moon Phase:	

Water

Temperature:	
Depth:	
Clarity:	
Speed:	
Direction:	
Notes:	

Tackle & Technique

Rod/Reel:

Bait:

Lures:

Fishing Method:

Notes:

Catch

Species	Length/Weight	Notes

Notes/Memories

Fishing Log

Date: | **Time:**

Location/GPS:

Fishing Crew:

Weather

Conditions:

Air Temp:

Wind Speed:

Wind Direction:

Barometer:

Moon Phase:

Water

Temperature:

Depth:

Clarity:

Speed:

Direction:

Notes:

Tackle & Technique

Rod/Reel:

Bait:

Lures:

Fishing Method:

Notes:

Catch

Species	Length/Weight	Notes

Notes/Memories

Fishing Log

Date:

Time:

Location/GPS:

Fishing Crew:

Weather

Conditions:

Air Temp:

Wind Speed:

Wind Direction:

Barometer:

Moon Phase:

Water

Temperature:

Depth:

Clarity:

Speed:

Direction:

Notes:

Tackle & Technique

Rod/Reel:

Bait:

Lures:

Fishing Method:

Notes:

Catch

Species	Length/Weight	Notes

Notes/Memories

Fishing Log

Date: | **Time:**

Location/GPS:

Fishing Crew:

Weather

Conditions:

Air Temp:

Wind Speed:

Wind Direction:

Barometer:

Moon Phase:

Water

Temperature:

Depth:

Clarity:

Speed:

Direction:

Notes:

Tackle & Technique

Rod/Reel:

Bait:

Lures:

Fishing Method:

Notes:

Catch

Species	Length/Weight	Notes

Notes/Memories

Fishing Log

Date: **Time:**

Location/GPS:

Fishing Crew:

Weather

Conditions:

Air Temp:

Wind Speed:

Wind Direction:

Barometer:

Moon Phase:

Water

Temperature:

Depth:

Clarity:

Speed:

Direction:

Notes:

Tackle & Technique

Rod/Reel:

Bait:

Lures:

Fishing Method:

Notes:

Catch

Species	Length/Weight	Notes

Notes/Memories

Fishing Log

Date: | **Time:**

Location/GPS:

Fishing Crew:

Weather

Conditions:

Air Temp:

Wind Speed:

Wind Direction:

Barometer:

Moon Phase:

Water

Temperature:

Depth:

Clarity:

Speed:

Direction:

Notes:

Tackle & Technique

Rod/Reel:

Bait:

Lures:

Fishing Method:

Notes:

Catch

Species	Length/Weight	Notes

Notes/Memories

Fishing Log

Date: | **Time:**

Location/GPS:

Fishing Crew:

Weather

Conditions:	
Air Temp:	
Wind Speed:	
Wind Direction:	
Barometer:	
Moon Phase:	

Water

Temperature:	
Depth:	
Clarity:	
Speed:	
Direction:	
Notes:	

Tackle & Technique

Rod/Reel:

Bait:

Lures:

Fishing Method:

Notes:

Catch

Species	Length/Weight	Notes

Notes/Memories

Fishing Log

Date: | **Time:**

Location/GPS:

Fishing Crew:

Weather

Conditions:

Air Temp:

Wind Speed:

Wind Direction:

Barometer:

Moon Phase:

Water

Temperature:

Depth:

Clarity:

Speed:

Direction:

Notes:

Tackle & Technique

Rod/Reel:

Bait:

Lures:

Fishing Method:

Notes:

Catch

Species	Length/Weight	Notes

Notes/Memories

Fishing Log

Date: | **Time:**

Location/GPS:

Fishing Crew:

Weather

Conditions:

Air Temp:

Wind Speed:

Wind Direction:

Barometer:

Moon Phase:

Water

Temperature:

Depth:

Clarity:

Speed:

Direction:

Notes:

Tackle & Technique

Rod/Reel:

Bait:

Lures:

Fishing Method:

Notes:

Catch

Species	Length/Weight	Notes

Notes/Memories

Fishing Log

Date: | **Time:**

Location/GPS:

Fishing Crew:

Weather

Conditions:	
Air Temp:	
Wind Speed:	
Wind Direction:	
Barometer:	
Moon Phase:	

Water

Temperature:	
Depth:	
Clarity:	
Speed:	
Direction:	
Notes:	

Tackle & Technique

Rod/Reel:

Bait:

Lures:

Fishing Method:

Notes:

Catch

Species	Length/Weight	Notes

Notes/Memories

Fishing Log

Date: | **Time:**

Location/GPS:

Fishing Crew:

Weather

Conditions:

Air Temp:

Wind Speed:

Wind Direction:

Barometer:

Moon Phase:

Water

Temperature:

Depth:

Clarity:

Speed:

Direction:

Notes:

Tackle & Technique

Rod/Reel:

Bait:

Lures:

Fishing Method:

Notes:

Catch

Species	Length/Weight	Notes

Notes/Memories

Fishing Log

Date:	Time:

Location/GPS:

Fishing Crew:

Weather

Conditions:
Air Temp:
Wind Speed:
Wind Direction:
Barometer:
Moon Phase:

Water

Temperature:
Depth:
Clarity:
Speed:
Direction:
Notes:

Tackle & Technique

Rod/Reel:
Bait:
Lures:
Fishing Method:
Notes:

Catch

Species	Length/Weight	Notes

Notes/Memories

Fishing Log

Date: | **Time:**

Location/GPS:

Fishing Crew:

Weather

Conditions:

Air Temp:

Wind Speed:

Wind Direction:

Barometer:

Moon Phase:

Water

Temperature:

Depth:

Clarity:

Speed:

Direction:

Notes:

Tackle & Technique

Rod/Reel:

Bait:

Lures:

Fishing Method:

Notes:

Catch

Species	Length/Weight	Notes

Notes/Memories

Fishing Log

Date: | **Time:**

Location/GPS:

Fishing Crew:

Weather

Conditions:

Air Temp:

Wind Speed:

Wind Direction:

Barometer:

Moon Phase:

Water

Temperature:

Depth:

Clarity:

Speed:

Direction:

Notes:

Tackle & Technique

Rod/Reel:

Bait:

Lures:

Fishing Method:

Notes:

Catch

Species	Length/Weight	Notes

Notes/Memories

_____

_____

_____

_____

_____

Fishing Log

Date: | **Time:**

Location/GPS:

Fishing Crew:

Weather

Conditions:

Air Temp:

Wind Speed:

Wind Direction:

Barometer:

Moon Phase:

Water

Temperature:

Depth:

Clarity:

Speed:

Direction:

Notes:

Tackle & Technique

Rod/Reel:

Bait:

Lures:

Fishing Method:

Notes:

Catch

Species	Length/Weight	Notes

Notes/Memories

Fishing Log

Date: | **Time:**

Location/GPS:

Fishing Crew:

Weather

Conditions:

Air Temp:

Wind Speed:

Wind Direction:

Barometer:

Moon Phase:

Water

Temperature:

Depth:

Clarity:

Speed:

Direction:

Notes:

Tackle & Technique

Rod/Reel:

Bait:

Lures:

Fishing Method:

Notes:

Catch

Species	Length/Weight	Notes

Notes/Memories

Fishing Log

Date: | **Time:**

Location/GPS:

Fishing Crew:

Weather

Conditions:

Air Temp:

Wind Speed:

Wind Direction:

Barometer:

Moon Phase:

Water

Temperature:

Depth:

Clarity:

Speed:

Direction:

Notes:

Tackle & Technique

Rod/Reel:

Bait:

Lures:

Fishing Method:

Notes:

Catch

Species	Length/Weight	Notes

Notes/Memories

Fishing Log

Date: | **Time:**

Location/GPS:

Fishing Crew:

Weather

Conditions:

Air Temp:

Wind Speed:

Wind Direction:

Barometer:

Moon Phase:

Water

Temperature:

Depth:

Clarity:

Speed:

Direction:

Notes:

Tackle & Technique

Rod/Reel:

Bait:

Lures:

Fishing Method:

Notes:

Catch

Species	Length/Weight	Notes

Notes/Memories

_____

_____

_____

_____

_____

_____

Fishing Log

Date: | **Time:**

Location/GPS:

Fishing Crew:

Weather

Conditions:

Air Temp:

Wind Speed:

Wind Direction:

Barometer:

Moon Phase:

Water

Temperature:

Depth:

Clarity:

Speed:

Direction:

Notes:

Tackle & Technique

Rod/Reel:

Bait:

Lures:

Fishing Method:

Notes:

Catch

Species	Length/Weight	Notes

Notes/Memories

Fishing Log

Date: | **Time:**

Location/GPS:

Fishing Crew:

Weather

Conditions:

Air Temp:

Wind Speed:

Wind Direction:

Barometer:

Moon Phase:

Water

Temperature:

Depth:

Clarity:

Speed:

Direction:

Notes:

Tackle & Technique

Rod/Reel:

Bait:

Lures:

Fishing Method:

Notes:

Catch

Species	Length/Weight	Notes

Notes/Memories

Fishing Log

Date: | **Time:**

Location/GPS:

Fishing Crew:

Weather

Conditions:

Air Temp:

Wind Speed:

Wind Direction:

Barometer:

Moon Phase:

Water

Temperature:

Depth:

Clarity:

Speed:

Direction:

Notes:

Tackle & Technique

Rod/Reel:

Bait:

Lures:

Fishing Method:

Notes:

Catch

Species	Length/Weight	Notes

Notes/Memories

Fishing Log

Date: | **Time:**

Location/GPS:

Fishing Crew:

Weather

Conditions:

Air Temp:

Wind Speed:

Wind Direction:

Barometer:

Moon Phase:

Water

Temperature:

Depth:

Clarity:

Speed:

Direction:

Notes:

Tackle & Technique

Rod/Reel:

Bait:

Lures:

Fishing Method:

Notes:

Catch

Species	Length/Weight	Notes

Notes/Memories

Fishing Log

Date: | **Time:**

Location/GPS:

Fishing Crew:

Weather

Conditions:

Air Temp:

Wind Speed:

Wind Direction:

Barometer:

Moon Phase:

Water

Temperature:

Depth:

Clarity:

Speed:

Direction:

Notes:

Tackle & Technique

Rod/Reel:

Bait:

Lures:

Fishing Method:

Notes:

Catch

Species	Length/Weight	Notes

Notes/Memories

Fishing Log

Date: | **Time:**

Location/GPS:

Fishing Crew:

Weather

Conditions:

Air Temp:

Wind Speed:

Wind Direction:

Barometer:

Moon Phase:

Water

Temperature:

Depth:

Clarity:

Speed:

Direction:

Notes:

Tackle & Technique

Rod/Reel:

Bait:

Lures:

Fishing Method:

Notes:

Catch

Species	Length/Weight	Notes

Notes/Memories

Fishing Log

Date:

Time:

Location/GPS:

Fishing Crew:

Weather

Conditions:

Air Temp:

Wind Speed:

Wind Direction:

Barometer:

Moon Phase:

Water

Temperature:

Depth:

Clarity:

Speed:

Direction:

Notes:

Tackle & Technique

Rod/Reel:

Bait:

Lures:

Fishing Method:

Notes:

Catch

Species	Length/Weight	Notes

Notes/Memories

_____

_____

_____

_____

_____

_____

Fishing Log

Date: | **Time:**

Location/GPS:

Fishing Crew:

Weather

Conditions:

Air Temp:

Wind Speed:

Wind Direction:

Barometer:

Moon Phase:

Water

Temperature:

Depth:

Clarity:

Speed:

Direction:

Notes:

Tackle & Technique

Rod/Reel:

Bait:

Lures:

Fishing Method:

Notes:

Catch

Species	Length/Weight	Notes

Notes/Memories

Fishing Log

Date: | **Time:**

Location/GPS:

Fishing Crew:

Weather

Conditions:	
Air Temp:	
Wind Speed:	
Wind Direction:	
Barometer:	
Moon Phase:	

Water

Temperature:	
Depth:	
Clarity:	
Speed:	
Direction:	
Notes:	

Tackle & Technique

Rod/Reel:

Bait:

Lures:

Fishing Method:

Notes:

Catch

Species	Length/Weight	Notes

Notes/Memories

Fishing Log

Date:

Time:

Location/GPS:

Fishing Crew:

Weather

Conditions:

Air Temp:

Wind Speed:

Wind Direction:

Barometer:

Moon Phase:

Water

Temperature:

Depth:

Clarity:

Speed:

Direction:

Notes:

Tackle & Technique

Rod/Reel:

Bait:

Lures:

Fishing Method:

Notes:

Catch

Species	Length/Weight	Notes

Notes/Memories

Fishing Log

Date: | **Time:**

Location/GPS:

Fishing Crew:

Weather

Conditions:	
Air Temp:	
Wind Speed:	
Wind Direction:	
Barometer:	
Moon Phase:	

Water

Temperature:	
Depth:	
Clarity:	
Speed:	
Direction:	
Notes:	

Tackle & Technique

Rod/Reel:

Bait:

Lures:

Fishing Method:

Notes:

Catch

Species	Length/Weight	Notes

Notes/Memories

Fishing Log

Date: | **Time:**

Location/GPS:

Fishing Crew:

Weather

Conditions:

Air Temp:

Wind Speed:

Wind Direction:

Barometer:

Moon Phase:

Water

Temperature:

Depth:

Clarity:

Speed:

Direction:

Notes:

Tackle & Technique

Rod/Reel:

Bait:

Lures:

Fishing Method:

Notes:

Catch

Species	Length/Weight	Notes

Notes/Memories

Fishing Log

Date: | **Time:**

Location/GPS:

Fishing Crew:

Weather

Conditions:

Air Temp:

Wind Speed:

Wind Direction:

Barometer:

Moon Phase:

Water

Temperature:

Depth:

Clarity:

Speed:

Direction:

Notes:

Tackle & Technique

Rod/Reel:

Bait:

Lures:

Fishing Method:

Notes:

Catch

Species	Length/Weight	Notes

Notes/Memories

Fishing Log

Date: | **Time:**

Location/GPS:

Fishing Crew:

Weather

Conditions:

Air Temp:

Wind Speed:

Wind Direction:

Barometer:

Moon Phase:

Water

Temperature:

Depth:

Clarity:

Speed:

Direction:

Notes:

Tackle & Technique

Rod/Reel:

Bait:

Lures:

Fishing Method:

Notes:

Catch

Species	Length/Weight	Notes

Notes/Memories

Fishing Log

Date: | **Time:**

Location/GPS:

Fishing Crew:

Weather

Conditions:	
Air Temp:	
Wind Speed:	
Wind Direction:	
Barometer:	
Moon Phase:	

Water

Temperature:	
Depth:	
Clarity:	
Speed:	
Direction:	
Notes:	

Tackle & Technique

Rod/Reel:

Bait:

Lures:

Fishing Method:

Notes:

Catch

Species	Length/Weight	Notes

Notes/Memories

Fishing Log

Date: | **Time:**

Location/GPS:

Fishing Crew:

Weather

Conditions:

Air Temp:

Wind Speed:

Wind Direction:

Barometer:

Moon Phase:

Water

Temperature:

Depth:

Clarity:

Speed:

Direction:

Notes:

Tackle & Technique

Rod/Reel:

Bait:

Lures:

Fishing Method:

Notes:

Catch

Species	Length/Weight	Notes

Notes/Memories

Fishing Log

Date: | **Time:**

Location/GPS:

Fishing Crew:

Weather

Conditions:	
Air Temp:	
Wind Speed:	
Wind Direction:	
Barometer:	
Moon Phase:	

Water

Temperature:	
Depth:	
Clarity:	
Speed:	
Direction:	
Notes:	

Tackle & Technique

Rod/Reel:	
Bait:	
Lures:	
Fishing Method:	
Notes:	

Catch

Species	Length/Weight	Notes

Notes/Memories

Fishing Log

Date: | **Time:**

Location/GPS:

Fishing Crew:

Weather

Conditions:

Air Temp:

Wind Speed:

Wind Direction:

Barometer:

Moon Phase:

Water

Temperature:

Depth:

Clarity:

Speed:

Direction:

Notes:

Tackle & Technique

Rod/Reel:

Bait:

Lures:

Fishing Method:

Notes:

Catch

Species	Length/Weight	Notes

Notes/Memories

Fishing Log

Date: | **Time:**

Location/GPS:

Fishing Crew:

Weather

Conditions:	
Air Temp:	
Wind Speed:	
Wind Direction:	
Barometer:	
Moon Phase:	

Water

Temperature:	
Depth:	
Clarity:	
Speed:	
Direction:	
Notes:	

Tackle & Technique

Rod/Reel:

Bait:

Lures:

Fishing Method:

Notes:

Catch

Species	Length/Weight	Notes

Notes/Memories

Fishing Log

Date: | **Time:**

Location/GPS:

Fishing Crew:

Weather

Conditions:	
Air Temp:	
Wind Speed:	
Wind Direction:	
Barometer:	
Moon Phase:	

Water

Temperature:	
Depth:	
Clarity:	
Speed:	
Direction:	
Notes:	

Tackle & Technique

Rod/Reel:

Bait:

Lures:

Fishing Method:

Notes:

Catch

Species	Length/Weight	Notes

Notes/Memories

Fishing Log

Date: | **Time:**

Location/GPS:

Fishing Crew:

Weather

Conditions:	
Air Temp:	
Wind Speed:	
Wind Direction:	
Barometer:	
Moon Phase:	

Water

Temperature:	
Depth:	
Clarity:	
Speed:	
Direction:	
Notes:	

Tackle & Technique

Rod/Reel:

Bait:

Lures:

Fishing Method:

Notes:

Catch

Species	Length/Weight	Notes

Notes/Memories

Fishing Log

Date: | **Time:**

Location/GPS:

Fishing Crew:

Weather

Conditions:

Air Temp:

Wind Speed:

Wind Direction:

Barometer:

Moon Phase:

Water

Temperature:

Depth:

Clarity:

Speed:

Direction:

Notes:

Tackle & Technique

Rod/Reel:

Bait:

Lures:

Fishing Method:

Notes:

Catch

Species	Length/Weight	Notes

Notes/Memories

Fishing Log

Date:

Time:

Location/GPS:

Fishing Crew:

Weather

Conditions:

Air Temp:

Wind Speed:

Wind Direction:

Barometer:

Moon Phase:

Water

Temperature:

Depth:

Clarity:

Speed:

Direction:

Notes:

Tackle & Technique

Rod/Reel:

Bait:

Lures:

Fishing Method:

Notes:

Catch

Species	Length/Weight	Notes

Notes/Memories

Fishing Log

Date: | **Time:**

Location/GPS:

Fishing Crew:

Weather

Conditions:

Air Temp:

Wind Speed:

Wind Direction:

Barometer:

Moon Phase:

Water

Temperature:

Depth:

Clarity:

Speed:

Direction:

Notes:

Tackle & Technique

Rod/Reel:

Bait:

Lures:

Fishing Method:

Notes:

Catch

Species	Length/Weight	Notes

Notes/Memories

Fishing Log

Date: | **Time:**

Location/GPS:

Fishing Crew:

Weather

Conditions:	
Air Temp:	
Wind Speed:	
Wind Direction:	
Barometer:	
Moon Phase:	

Water

Temperature:	
Depth:	
Clarity:	
Speed:	
Direction:	
Notes:	

Tackle & Technique

Rod/Reel:

Bait:

Lures:

Fishing Method:

Notes:

Catch

Species	Length/Weight	Notes

Notes/Memories

Fishing Log

Date:

Time:

Location/GPS:

Fishing Crew:

Weather

Conditions:

Air Temp:

Wind Speed:

Wind Direction:

Barometer:

Moon Phase:

Water

Temperature:

Depth:

Clarity:

Speed:

Direction:

Notes:

Tackle & Technique

Rod/Reel:

Bait:

Lures:

Fishing Method:

Notes:

Catch

Species	Length/Weight	Notes

Notes/Memories

_____

_____

_____

_____

_____

_____

Fishing Log

Date: | **Time:**

Location/GPS:

Fishing Crew:

Weather

Conditions:

Air Temp:

Wind Speed:

Wind Direction:

Barometer:

Moon Phase:

Water

Temperature:

Depth:

Clarity:

Speed:

Direction:

Notes:

Tackle & Technique

Rod/Reel:

Bait:

Lures:

Fishing Method:

Notes:

Catch

Species	Length/Weight	Notes

Notes/Memories

Fishing Log

Date: | **Time:**

Location/GPS:

Fishing Crew:

Weather

Conditions:

Air Temp:

Wind Speed:

Wind Direction:

Barometer:

Moon Phase:

Water

Temperature:

Depth:

Clarity:

Speed:

Direction:

Notes:

Tackle & Technique

Rod/Reel:

Bait:

Lures:

Fishing Method:

Notes:

Catch

Species	Length/Weight	Notes

Notes/Memories

Fishing Log

Date: | **Time:**

Location/GPS:

Fishing Crew:

Weather

Conditions:	
Air Temp:	
Wind Speed:	
Wind Direction:	
Barometer:	
Moon Phase:	

Water

Temperature:	
Depth:	
Clarity:	
Speed:	
Direction:	
Notes:	

Tackle & Technique

Rod/Reel:

Bait:

Lures:

Fishing Method:

Notes:

Catch

Species	Length/Weight	Notes

Notes/Memories